Higher than Happiness

by

Michael Kewley
Dhammachariya Paññadipa

All rights reserved.

No part of this publication may be reproduced, stored in a retrieval system or transmitted, in any form or by any means, electronic, mechanical, photocopying, recording or otherwise, without prior permission of the publishers.

This book is sold subject to the condition that it shall not by way of trade or otherwise, be lent, re-sold, hired out or otherwise circulated without the publishers prior consent in any form of binding cover other than that in which it is published and without similar condition including this condition being imposed on the subsequent purchaser.

Copyright © Michael Kewley 1994
ISBN: 1-899417-00-1

Revised edition 2014
ISBN: 978-1-899417-17-9

Published by:
Pannadipa Books.
e-mail:
dhammateacher@hotmail.com

Cover photo by Pascal Gauthier

Dedication

To my father,
my first teacher.

Introduction

It has been a beautiful realisation for me to recognise that my father was actually my hero and first spiritual guide. His influence in my life was something that was always to my benefit.

Growing up in the nineteen sixties, as I did there were many times when my father and I would argue. Perhaps argue is too mild a word. There were ferocious battles of will, each certain that the other was wrong and that we were right. There was never any compromise.

This was a time of great change in society and the generation gap was never wider. New and revolutionary ideas colliding headlong into past conditioning. Long hair, freedom of speech, exotic clothes and music and an interest in new and unusual ways of living. Parents in that time seemed to be old fashioned, firmly established in the past and unwilling to change or even listen to what we had to say. They were most definitely unenlightened.

To think that I could be influenced by one of them seemed to me to be completely out of character.

My father was basically a simple and joyful man who wanted a quiet life. He made no secret of that. He liked things ordered and to run smoothly. He was unpretentious, proud of his working-class roots and had two philosophies is that he lived by.

The first was, 'Keep it Simple'.

Although he was a highly intelligent man he knew the value of simplicity in all his dealings and had the ability to strip the situation down to its bare bones and to keep it there. No long intellectual discussions for him, it was always straight to the heart of the matter. He knew what was important and what wasn't and how to cut away the excess.

The second philosophy was, 'Act stupid'.

By this he meant be ready to learn. Don't think you know everything when you don't. Be humble. There is always someone with greater experience and knowledge than you, whatever aspect of life you look at.

Without realising it these two philosophies began to influence me and I see them now as an indication of wisdom.
Of course, when I was young I missed the point, but as the old saying goes, 'When I was eighteen my father knew nothing, but by the time I was twenty five he had learned a lot.'

In my spiritual pursuit, I have been blessed by meeting, working and training with only the best teachers. I feel very privileged to have been in their presence and received instruction from them, but now I see that in principle, their teaching is exactly the same as my father's, 'Keep it simple and act stupid.'

For any living being, the experience of truth
is truly a blessing for the whole world.
May we all discover its essential simplicity
and learn to live in humility.

May all beings be happy

Higher Than Happiness

Contents

The truth is in no special place
Everything is practice
Sweeping the leaves
Magic or wisdom?
Not today
Don't defend yourself
Looking at ourselves
Love openly
Keep it simple
The empty mind
Living in the sunshine
No-one can do it for you
Higher than happiness
Muddy road
Humility
Super illusion
Simple daily meditation

Higher Than Happiness

The truth is in no special place
'In every moment the opportunity for spiritual development is presenting itself.'

At the time of the Buddha there was also a being known as Monkey living in India. Monkey had special powers and because of this, a lot of conceit. He felt himself to be greater even than the Buddha, and so set out to prove this point.

He challenged the Buddha to a contest to compare their respective abilities.

"Well," said the Buddha, "what can you do?"

"I can spin somersaults to the end of the universe," boasted Monkey, "and that makes me greater than you."

"Please show me," said the Buddha.

Monkey performed a few practice leaps, spinning in the air before landing and then, when he had finally prepared himself, leapt as hard as he could and disappeared into the clouds. On and on he spun somersaulting through space until finally he arrived at the end of the universe.

The end of the universe was marked by five great columns and Monkey sat down at the foot of the middle one to rest. 'I had better do something to prove I was here,' he thought, and so taking a pencil, wrote his name down the centre of the fourth column.

When he had rested for as long as he needed, he relieved himself under his name and set off back to earth to see the Buddha.

"There," he said upon his return, "I did it."
"How can I be sure you have done what you claim?" asked the Buddha.
"Aha," exclaimed Monkey, "I knew that you'd ask that, so I wrote my name down the middle of the fourth column and relieved myself underneath it. That will prove I was there."
"Like this?" asked the Buddha and opened his hand to reveal Monkey's name written down his fourth finger, and a few drops of golden liquid beneath it.
Monkey then realised his power was no match for the Buddha.

It is true that when many people begin spiritual practice they believe that they have found something special, something exclusive, something separate from ordinary life. In fact, they may go to great lengths to change everything about their lives and the way they live. Wearing special clothes, dressing their hair in certain ways and even performing particular ceremonies and meditations in order to change themselves. Often, however, this will only serve to cause upset and division with their family, friends and partners. This is not uncommon, and is in reality, just a sign of spiritual immaturity. Separating ordinary life from the spiritual path.

The goal of spiritual pursuit is wisdom, the arising of insight, and the ability to live peacefully in the world whatever circumstances present themselves. Balance and harmony are the two outward manifestations of this wisdom. Attempting to create only certain, preconceived conditions for spiritual development is doomed to failure, and can only result in frustration and disappointment. If spiritual practice is to have any real and lasting value it must include everything, every aspect of life.

As our understanding deepens, we can see that nothing is outside Dhamma.
Dhamma is a Buddhist word that means ultimate truth. From ultimate truth everything arises. All good things and all the bad. Nothing is an exception to this.
We don't need to get rid of all our possessions, but we do need to examine our attachment to them. We don't need to get rid of our family and friends, but we do need to understand our resentment towards them. With the arising of wisdom, we can recognise that all the things we thought were obstacles to personal development are in fact, the very things that will lead as to it.

Life is an unfolding process. In it we can often experience much pleasure. Being with loved ones, feeling happy with our circumstances and generally being at ease. Through our practice of insight and loving kindness meditation we are able to enjoy these things while they last but not despair when they change. Nothing lasts forever, and as long as we cling to pleasant conditions, we will all be subject to disappointment and pain when they change.
Life is also subject to many painful conditions and events. The ending of a relationship, the death of a loved one, or just the general feelings of stress, anxiety and unhappiness, are experiences all of us will have to bear. But these too, viewed through the eyes of wisdom can be seen as objects for reflection. Everything that begins must end. This is a universal law, and wisdom means to understand this at the intuitive level. Once we have wisdom, we are able to

live within the changing and uncontrolled conditions of life in a calm and balanced way. Having the openness to enjoy what can be enjoyed, and the fortitude to endure that which has to be endured.

Seeing everything as clouds passing through a perfect sky, sometimes obscuring the sun, but always moving on. We need to ask ourselves what is the result of my spiritual efforts? What is the fruit of my practice?
If our life is not becoming easier and happier we are doing something wrong, we are still caught in the trap of trying to make everything perfect for ourselves and blaming other people and conditions when things don't go our way. With this view, we are dividing our life. We are struggling with life. We are the victim of life, because we have no real control of our own.

Allow everything to act in accordance with its nature and be easy. When we let go of struggle peace arises. We don't need to create it within ourselves, we only have to allow the obstacles to it fall away.

Nothing is an obstacle to practice and so nothing is outside it. In every moment the opportunity for spiritual development is presenting itself.

Even if we could somersault to the end of the universe, we would still be within the realm and Dhamma, of wisdom. Use wisdom to develop wisdom. Let your practice be all-inclusive. Relax, be open and let the fruits of your efforts multiply.

Everything is practice
'Let go of choice and be with what is.'

A young physician went to a Dhamma Master and asked to be taught Dhamma.

"Dhamma is not such a difficult practice," said the Master. "if you are physician, treat your patients with kindness, that is Dhamma."

The physician visited the Master three times and on each occasion he was told the same thing. The Master would say, "A physician should not waste his time here, go home and take care of your patients."

It was not clear how such a teaching could remove the doubts and confusion about life that the young physician had and so on the fourth visit he complained to the Master. The Master smiled and said, "Perhaps I have been too hard on you. I will give you a meditation to practice." He instructed the physician in Vipassana meditation.

The physician practiced this form of meditation ardently each day for two years. At length the thought he had attained clarity of mind, but the Master commented, "You are not there yet."

The physician continued to practice. In time his mind became calm and balanced. Problems and doubts dissolved. Emptiness became the truth for him. He served his patients well and without ever knowing it, became free from the concern of life and death. The next time he visited the Master, the Master simply smiled.

It is a recurrent theme of mine that spiritual life is ordinary life. There is no separation between the two. To progress in spiritual understanding there is no need to renounce the world, to give up the ordinary things of life and lock yourself away in a cave or a monastery, to cut yourself off from the world. There is no requirement to become a monk or a nun or a recluse. Living in the world is excellent practice.

For many years I worked in a factory alongside six hundred others. Factory life is difficult for many people and is seen to encourage the lowest aspects of mind. It is the same with all work that seems pointless and empty. Pettiness, mental dullness and irritation are common. So is back biting, tale bearing and gossip. However, these are the things that fill the day and break the most overpowering mental state of all, that of boredom. Boredom with the work, boredom with the people, and boredom with life. I rarely met people enthusiastic about their job. To be in a situation like this can be very testing, soul destroying in fact, but in spiritual training we must remember that everything depends upon attitude.

If you're doing something that you don't want to do then everything connected with it becomes a drudge. Having to work in such conditions can seem like a prison sentence, but if you see this as an opportunity to train and develop everything will change for you.

No more drudge, no more complaint, just the opportunity to practice.

When things go well there is the moment for you to see the mind and its reactions. When things do not go well, there is the same opportunity. It all depends on attitude. Do you see this as an opportunity to practice or not?

If you say yes, there are no more problems for you, everything changes. However, if you say no, right there in that answer is the arising of unhappiness. Unhappiness begins in the mind of the person who always wants everything to go his or her own and very limited way.

I was very fortunate in my time at the factory. I would begin each day with meditation, and go to work, meditate at lunchtime, continue work, go home and meditate again. I had formal meditation and working meditation. What an opportunity to train. Being with so many people, all very different to me, was the opportunity to watch myself, to watch the mind. Upon reflection, I value my time of the factory very much. I learned a lot about myself, this ego and how it manifests and most importantly, how to surrender. When there is no choice the only thing to do is to surrender, to be open and learn. I have lived in a monastery and worked in a factory, I do not want to say which was the greatest teacher, both had their own value and their own place in my life.

We cannot always choose the conditions we live under. No matter how hard we try, we are not able to make everything perfect according to our desires, and as long as we attempt to do this we will surely suffer.

Look at the world. Look how everyone follows this path, and look at the results when they fail. Misery, anger and unhappiness. From the position of practice everything is perfect, just as it is. There are no special conditions we have to create and nothing special that we have to do. Whether we work in a factory, a shop, an office or stay at home and look after our family, right there are the perfect conditions for practice. There is nothing outside mind and body and so nothing is outside our practice.

Let go of the desire to make everything the way you think that it should be and be with things as they are. Look at your mind, your feelings, your reactions, your happiness and your unhappiness and right there is your practice. Learn to be open, accepting and responsive. This is the practice of the enlightened mind. Choosing one thing over another is the foundation of unhappiness. Let go of choice and be with what is.

In life, we all have to experience many different conditions, some good, some not so good, some downright painful! All of us are subject to the whole range of human emotions and feelings. It is the same for everyone. Pleasure and pain arise endlessly, and as long as we are attached to one of the other we will suffer.

As one ancient Dhamma Master has said,

The Great Way is simple, it only means giving up picking and choosing.

Usually, we would prefer pleasant bodily sensations to their opposites, but the story of the man in hospital might help us to let go, even of this choice.

He had awoken at home in the early morning with severe pain in his abdomen. This became increasingly worse as the morning progressed and finally a doctor was called. The doctor suspected kidney stones and so sent him to hospital for an examination. Once in the hospital still waiting to be seen and the pain intensifying each minute, the man, in a moment of desperation, heard himself exclaim 'Jesus

Christ take this pain away!'
Then, from somewhere in the back of his mind a quiet gentle loving voice replied, "Take it away, I've only just given it to you?"

Everything is the opportunity for practice, the painful experiences as well as the pleasant.
Learn to look at your life as the gift that it is. The opportunity to attain full enlightenment, the end of all your suffering and unhappiness and cultivate a mind that will use every waking moment to achieve it.

Sweeping the leaves
'Everything we experience happens within our mind.'

At one time a young monk was asked to look after an old, almost derelict temple in the hills in Japan. He felt pleased to do this as his nature was already to be precise in his actions and so this would be an opportunity for him to make something from nothing. To renovate an old building and then have it exactly the way he wanted it to be.

Living alongside the temple was an old enlightened Master. He had retired from teaching and enjoyed the peace of a quiet life. One of the young monks duties was to look after this Master, to prepare his food and to attend to his needs. One day a message was received that the young monk was to expect a visit from his superiors, who would assess the work he had done in the temple.

All morning, he worked hard, cleaning and preparing for the visit. He wanted everywhere to look as good as it could. Finally, there was just one job left.

The night before there had been a strong wind and the garden was strewn with leaves that had blown down from the tree standing in the centre of the lawn. The young monk took his wooden broom and began to sweep. Carefully gathering of fallen leaves together, he put them in a sack and removed them from the garden, all the while watched by the Master, who was leaning on the adjoining fence. When the very last leaf had been carried away, the young monk turned to the Master and asked him what he thought.

"Not bad, not bad," said the Master, "there is just one thing needed to make it perfect."

The young monk was hesitant. He had done everything he could think of what more could there be?

"Just help me over the fence and I'll show you," continued the Master.

Reluctantly, the young monk obeyed. He had come to know this Master, and knew to expect the unexpected. The Master, once in the temple grounds, staggered over to the tree in the centre of the garden, and with all the strength in his frail old body shook it as hard as he could. The remaining leaves fluttered down onto the lawn falling into a haphazard pattern. As the young monk's superiors could be seen climbing the hill to the temple the Master turned to him and said, "Now, everything is perfect!"

We all have a perception of perfection. We carry with us an idea of how everything should be and because of this spend huge amounts of time and energy trying to arrange conditions to match this idea. Our family, friends, partners and colleagues, our work and social engagements. Nothing falls outside our desire to be happy by controlling all the things we think we need to produce that happiness. It is a constant struggle.

The blueprint for perfection against the realities of life.

However perfection, as it is usually understood, is just an idea. It is a concept, and not only can it not be realised in any real and lasting way, our perception of it is always changing anyway.

What made us happy once may not have the same effect a second time and so we change our requirements. Our mind is always moving. Thoughts, feelings, moods and emotions come and go without end, and so what was necessary in any particular moment to fulfil our concept of perfection is always changing and adjusting itself to fit our needs and desires.

And even if we do manage to contrive and manipulate a situation where everything seems to be perfect, there is always something that interferes with it. A telephone call when we finally managed to sink into a hot bath at the end of a long hard day, or the need to get up and make a cup of tea when we are relaxing, or simply having to go to the toilet in the middle of our favourite television programme. The perfect state, even if it can be touched, is fleeting.

Meditation practice can be like this. Trying to arrange circumstances, so that they are perfect for us. A time when we can be alone, in comfortable surroundings, and not be disturbed. Then we can really get on with our practice. Then we can really watch the mind. But the mind that we see in meditation is not a special mind. It is not something that only appears when we sit quietly. It is the mind that is always with us. Sitting quietly or not, it comes and goes by itself, filled with thoughts, distractions, pleasant feelings and unpleasant feelings - and the desire to make everything perfect!

If we are dedicated to the spiritual path of self investigation, we have to realise that whether we are sitting in meditation or not, this awareness practice can still continue. Physical posture in the end, counts for very little.

At one time in India, a young teacher trained in a religious form of Buddhism was asked if it was possible for whales and dolphins to become enlightened. These are highly intelligent creatures, and so the question seemed a valid one to the student.

However, after a long pause, the teacher answered, "No whales and dolphins cannot become enlightened, because they are not able to sit in the full lotus posture, and they cannot bow to the Buddha."

It is better to be silent than to give such an answer as this.

The Buddha said that awareness is everything.

To notice the nature of the mind and to be at peace with it is the fruit of this practice. Not constantly seeking to fulfil a limited idea of how everything should be but be at peace with things as they are, creates perfect practice. Of course this attitude demands something from us. It demands surrender.

In common usage, the word surrender means to reluctantly give up something that we really want. We feel the need to hold on to a particular object, an idea, or feeling, or emotion and because of circumstances beyond our control, it is being taken away from us. Like soldiers on a battlefield, when the bullets have all been fired there is no choice but to give in. To surrender.

However, in spiritual terms surrender means something different. It means to let go. To be in harmony. To give up the struggle with life and to be easy. Making choices and decisions when they are available, but not suffering when we have to accept circumstances we cannot change. Surrender means to be centred. To be in control of our life. Real control. Not of the external world, but of the internal world. Of our responses and reactions.

Everything we experience happens within our mind. Anger, fear, frustration and all our negative mental states begin and end within us. No one gives them to us and no one can take them away. We do it to ourselves. As we begin to understand this, we can peacefully let them go. Not attempting to drive them away with an attitude of, 'I shouldn't feel like this,' but to see them for what they really are, impersonal movements of mind, not 'me,' not 'mine,' not what 'I am'.

They are like visitors to your house. Perhaps you don't like them, but you can still be kind and polite. You don't have to ask them to stay, but you don't need to throw them out either. Eventually, and without any fuss, they will grow tired and leave by themselves.

Happiness is the same. It begins and ends within us. No one gives it to us and no one can take it away. But if we feel we are dependent upon certain circumstances for our happiness, then it can always be lost. Someone or something can take it away from us.

This type of happiness, established in our quest for perfection, is truly superficial and naturally has no sustaining power. If someone can give it then someone can take it away again.

True happiness comes from Dhamma. When peace and acceptance are our starting points, everything else flows. Whatever the circumstances, we can be happy. Not trying to create a world where everything is the way we think it should be, but being at peace with things as they are.

No fight. No struggle.

The leaves falling from the tree is not the problem. Seeing them on the ground and wishing they were not there is the problem.
Whether others see things our way or not is not the problem, feeling the need to make them do so is the problem.

Open your heart through practice, letting go of the desire to create a perfect world for your self, and be easy. Perfection is only an idea anyway. It only truly exists when we see that everything is already perfect, just as it is.

Magic or wisdom?
'If we want to remove unhappiness from our lives, we have to remove ignorance.'

Once, when a Dhamma Master was teaching at a certain temple, a follower from another tradition was in the audience and began to cause a disturbance. Because he was so jealous of this Masters reputation he sought to discredit him, by engaging in a debate.

The Master eventually invited the man to the front of the crowd and allowed him to speak.

"The founder of our sect has such miraculous powers," began the man, "that if he stood on one bank of the river and wrote letters in the air, they would appear on a piece of paper held by an attendant on the other bank. Can you do such a wonderful thing?"

"Perhaps your fox can perform that sort of magic," said the Master, "but that is not the way of true Dhamma. My magic is that when I eat, I really eat, and when I drink, I really drink!"

There is a common fascination with magic and the attainment of miraculous powers. Many people involve themselves in so-called 'spiritual practice' for just such reasons. The development of special powers such as magic and healing sets one apart from others and is generally understood as being synonymous with spiritual progress. However, for true spiritual practitioners, the acquisition of magical powers can actually be seen as a hindrance. An obstacle to the truth.

The reality is to be more balanced, relaxed and open. If they occur naturally, all well and good, but if one actively seeks them, look at your motives. Who exactly wants what?

Many years ago before discovering meditation, I became very interested in astral projection. I was fascinated by the idea that one could leave one's own body and not only travel in this world, but also visit other planes of existence. I bought and read many books on the subject and spent perhaps hundreds of hours practising the exercises and techniques I had read. All to no avail. I never went anywhere, and eventually I gave up trying.

But I was interested - for a while.

Actually, it's not surprising that people from our culture have a specific interest in magic, when you remember Jesus and the Bible stories. The miracles form an important part of the Christian belief system and to most people are what Jesus is actually remembered for. Walking on water, raising the dead and turning water into wine.

The teaching itself come second to the miracles, which are seen as the proof of the divinity of Christ.

There was once a Master telling a story to a student to curb his interest in acquiring special or magical powers.

The story was about another Master, who wanted to cross a river. He approached the boatman and asked him to ferry him across.

"That will cost you one penny," said the boatman.

"But I don't have a penny," replied that Master.
"Then I won't take you across," said the boatman.
On hearing those words, the Master stepped off the bank of the river and walked across on the water.

The Master who was telling this story, explained to his student that such a trick is not even worth the penny he should have paid the boatman in the first place.
Such is a Masters understanding of the value of magic.
Perhaps a modern variation of this story is this:

Sometime ago a person asked me if they could look at one of my books.
Naturally, I said yes and I offered it to him. He held the book in his hand from moment, and I asked with a smile, "Would you like to buy it?"
He took a small box from his pocket and having opened it, removed a pendulum from inside. He held the pendulum over the book for a moment, and it began to move. He then looked at me and said, "No I won't buy the book," and walked away.

Perhaps this sounds impressive to you, but we need to reflect. If we are not able to buy even a book without the use of a pendulum are we really free in our lives?

Although magic and special powers can be impressive, they do not necessarily indicate wisdom, and it is only wisdom, that will save ourselves and the world that we live in. As long as there is no wisdom there is an abundance of ignorance, and ignorance always means confusion for ourselves and others. Couple that with magical powers,

and there can really be a dangerous situation.
Ego, that part of us that needs to be seen as someone special, someone different from the crowd, can lead us to act in a way that will bring only harm, no matter how noble or pure minded we think our actions are.
As long as there is ego there is always the danger of abuse.

So what can be done?

All spiritual tradition speak of magic, but all Masters dismiss it as irrelevant. It's just not important. It's not an indication of anything!

The real magic in spiritual practice is the intuitive understanding of mind and body. Of knowing ourselves by realising the nature of our reality. Of being balanced and at peace, whatever is happening. Of living a life established in love, and awareness.

There is another story of a Master, whose monastery was being attacked by an invading force.

The Master sat in meditation, untroubled by what was happening until he was at last disturbed by the leader of the attackers who placed the point of his sword at the base of his throat and proudly said, "I am one who can run you through without batting an eyelid."
"And I sir," replied the Master, "am one who can be run through without batting an eyelid."

This is real magic, complete equanimity established in a deep experience and intuitive understanding of reality.

How could this man ever be defeated?

As one turns inward more and more through the development of a calm and peaceful mind, one's own abilities naturally develop.

All of us can recognise anger in another. It's not usually very difficult to see, even if that person is actively trying not to show it. Always something, some gesture or phrase betrays them. However, from the perspective of the meditative mind, our ability to recognise even the most subtle mental states of others becomes greatly sharpened as we ourselves become more sensitive and less ego based.

Less outward projection into the world, and more balance.

Perhaps you could call this 'mind reading', a magical power, but in reality, it is just an opening of ourselves. Being receptive to the mind of another without enforcing our will onto situation. Allowing others to show themselves.

We have to understand that the cause of our unhappiness, however we define it, is ourselves and nothing, not even the attainment of magical powers, will alter that. The whole of the Buddhist teaching revolves around this point. All of our unhappiness and struggle with life is caused by desire and craving, wanting things to be other than they are, and these have their roots in ignorance. If we want to remove unhappiness from our lives we have to remove ignorance. Nothing else will do it.

Nothing!

The central theme of true spiritual training is the removing of ignorance by knowing the mind and body as they really are and not trying to develop special powers. It is our continual identification with the delusion of 'self', that is the cause of all our problems and difficulties in life, and not even being able to walk on water or through walls will change this.

The real magic in life is in wisdom, and real power lies in the non-attachment to the mind and body complex that we call 'self'. If you truly want to develop yourself, follow the way of wisdom. Wisdom leads to peace and happiness and from that everyone benefits.

The Master in the story at the beginning knew where real power lay. Not in magical tricks and displays, but in simply being with the ordinary things of life. In giving full attention to the act of eating and drinking, and everything else he was involved in. This is real ability and will without doubt lead to the overcoming of sorrow and unhappiness and the desire to be someone special. It will lead to the realisation of truth and the complete knowing of oneself.

Not today
'Death will occur and we don't know when.'

At one time there was a flock of sheep, who lived in a meadow. One day a rumour began that the farmer was going to kill them all, so one sheep was elected to go to the farmer and ask if this was true.
After some time the sheep returned to the meadow, skipping and hopping and smiling broadly.
"Well," said the rest of the flock, "is he going to kill us?"
"Yes," replied the sheep, "but not today."

It is true that death faces us all. It is inescapable. From the moment we are born it is the only thing we can know with any real certainty, and as much as we may want things to be otherwise, it is completely beyond our control.
We can do many things to improve the quality of our life, such as exercise, eating good food and even involving ourselves in meditation or other spiritual practices, but at some point all this must end. Death will come no matter what we do. No one can live forever, and everyone who is born has to die.

I have heard that in Ireland there are a group of people who believe that death is conditioned solely by thinking about it, and if it is never thought about, or brought up in conversation, it just won't happen.
This is their philosophy, and if it turns out to be true, and

they don't die, they will be the first people ever to live and not have to face their own death.

Even enlightened beings have had to die. The Buddha died at eighty, and according to the Christian tradition, Jesus was thirty three years old. Even Methuselah, in the Bible, had to die. He lived until he was more than seven hundred years old, but in one moment it was over. Death occurred, and nothing more could be done.

And it can happen at any time. Look around you. People die young. Babies die, children die, adolescents and young adults die. It is not only the old that have to face death. From the moment we are born, it is the only sure thing in life.

Death will occur, and we don't know when.

But not today.

At least, not in this moment.

In this moment we are alive.

Right now we have life, and right now we have the best possible opportunity of living it to the full. Of making the most of every second there is.

Of course, in spiritual terms, living life to the full does not mean going to parties, drinking alcohol or taking other drugs. It does not mean using other people for our own advantage, sexually or otherwise, or taking objects that belong to them. It means seizing with a passion, every moment as the opportunity to develop further and further in the path of love and wisdom.

Life is so precious that not to use it in this way is simply a waste!

As we deepen the understanding of ourselves through the practice of Insight and Loving Kindness Meditation (Vipassana and Metta Bhavana), we begin to see and appreciate the value of life. Our past habits and conditioning become revealed to us, are accepted without comment or judgement and then allowed to simply fall away. The resultant clarity of the now open and spacious mind provides the condition for the experience of life to be fully understood.

Not to use others but to be of use. Not to harm others but to be gentle and kind. Not to be confused by the appearance of things, but to use every moment to allow the truth to arise within us.

This is how we can learn to live to our limitless limit. To live life to the full.

Unpleasant mental states come and go by themselves, so do the pleasant ones, like clouds passing through a clear sky. Not 'me', not 'mine' and not what 'I am'. Only mind moving.

The more we are able to experience this simple truth with loving awareness, the more complete will be our liberation from the trap of the mind. When we are free from this trap, we are free from even the thought of life and death.

One teacher has said, 'No one was ever born and no one will ever die, it just looks like that!' Once we can fully understand this truth, not with the intellect but with the intuitive mind, the spiritual heart, we are liberated forever from the distinction between life and death.

So when you are alive, live.

Don't waste a moment. Don't die before you learn how to make the most of this precious time.
This is the opportunity of life.

Many people ask me, 'What is the purpose of life?'
I always give the same reply, 'There is no purpose to life'.

There is no cosmic scheme behind our existence. No superior being directing us or ordaining certain events for us. Everything is entirely in our own hands. Life as we experience it is a consequence. It is the result of something that has gone before.

However, if there is no inherent purpose to life, it is a rare and special opportunity. It is the opportunity for the liberation from our unhappiness.
According to Buddhist teachings only human beings can realise enlightenment. The gods or so-called 'higher beings' can't do it, neither can the beings in the animal or ghostly kingdoms. Only human beings have the opportunity and capability to fully know themselves and so be liberated from the realms of suffering and unhappiness.

Right now you have this opportunity and capability. What will you do with it?

To say, 'I will start tomorrow', maybe leaving it too late,

and next year or even next week may never come for you.

Don't allow this chance to slip by. Only you can cultivate your life so that it becomes a blessing for yourself and for the world, as beautiful as a lotus flower growing in a muddy pool.

Death will come to you, that is for sure.
But not today.

Don't miss this moment!

Don't defend yourself
'Conforming makes everyone's life more comfortable.'

Zen students take a vow that even if they are killed by the teacher their intention is to truly learn the Dhamma. This has now become just a formality and is usually declared by the cutting of a finger. However, in olden times it was a completely different matter.

Eikido had become a stern master, and all of his students feared him. One day a student striking a gong to tell the time of day, missed a beat when his eye was attracted by beautiful girl passing by the temple gate. At that moment Eikido, who was standing directly behind him, hit the student on the head with his stick.
The shock of the blow killed the student outright!
The guardian of the dead boy, hearing of the incident, went immediately to Eikido. Knowing he was not to blame, he praised the master for his severe teaching. Eikido's attitude was just the same as if the student was still alive.
After this took place Eikido was able to produce more than ten enlightened successors, a very unusual number.

Our usual way of being is to live in accordance with the rules and regulations set down by others. To play other people's games. They tell us what is right and what is wrong, and most importantly, how we should behave. This is simply conditioning by our parents, our educational system and society in general. At a very early age we learn that certain modes of behaviour are either acceptable or not. We loose spontaneous action, because in our mind we always trapped by this conditioning.

A student of mine telephoned me one day to ask a question. She had been in a relationship with a man which had ended and was now seeing someone else. The first man had met her unexpectedly one day, and expressed the desire to rekindle their involvement with each other. However, there was a condition. She had to stop seeing the other man. He told her that she must choose, one or the other.
My friend was confused. She liked them both, what should she do?
I told her that she didn't have to do anything. Making a choice between the two men in her life was someone else's game, and she didn't have to play. If she wanted to see one, or the other, or neither or both, that was a choice that she could make. There was no need for her to feel forced into situation by the demands of someone else. She was free to make her own decision. To live her own life.

This is how it is for most of us. We find ourselves dragged into playing other people's games. Even if we don't want to, because of our past conditioning, we find it hard to resist and therefore live our life according to the demands of others. We never fully experience a sense of freedom, because of continual external pressure from parents, friends, family and the rest of society. They all know how we should be and if we resist their view of life, they turn up the pressure.

Conforming makes everyone's life more comfortable.

To live a spiritual life means to stop playing this game. To be your own person. It does not mean however, that we just become more selfish and self-centred completely disregarding the feelings of others. On the contrary, through the investigation of mind and body we develop and then continue to develop, a less selfish view of ourselves and the world that we live in. We become more open and harmonious to the feelings of others. But, from the position of selflessness and balance, we can see impartially what needs to be done and what needs to be left undone. We are no longer swayed by opinion. We do what is right to do.

In order to reach this stage of being we have to let go of our usual and habitual need to see ourselves, and be seen by others, in a certain light. To continually reinforce the idea that we are nice people, and therefore only capable of good actions. We have to learn to be open to ourselves, however, we are.
With this comes confidence, not conceit. Not the idea that only we know what is best for everyone, but the knowledge that each must make their own way in the world as is appropriate for them. We can help of course, be of service, but never be compromised by the opinion of others. This means that what others think of us means nothing. Everyone is criticised from time to time. Look at the lives of Jesus and the Buddha. Both were enlightened and both were subject to many criticisms from the unenlightened. However, the opinions of others did not concern them. Their only concern was the truth, and how to express it best.

When we embark upon a spiritual life we have to develop purity. This is what the spiritual life truly means, a pure life. However, at the beginning we may need to follow certain rules of training, guidelines that will help us cultivate this purity.

These rules are fundamental to progress along the spiritual path and discourage killing or inflicting pain or harm on other beings, stealing, using our speech in wrong and harmful ways, sexual misconduct and the use of drinks and drugs that tend to cloud the mind.

But these guidelines should not be seen as acts of repression. We have to investigate and understand the outcome of such acts and realise that not only do the victims suffer, but that we also suffer.

All breaches of morality stem from ego, from the desire to create and maintain perfect conditions of life for ourselves. It is exactly this motivation that we have to let go of.

Our morality must be a natural morality, arising from a pure heart, a pure centre. This can only happen when our intention is to train ourselves in the way of an enlightened being.

It is said that the moral training of the Buddhist is simply the way an enlightened being behaves naturally in the world. We act as though we are already enlightened in harmony with all beings.

One time, when I was in India, staying in the small town of Banda, I was asked about killing mosquitoes.

Now I, like everyone else, do not like mosquitoes very much. I don't like them on me and I certainly do not like them to bite me. However, the desire to kill them simply does not arise. I will blow them off gently or brush them off with my hand, but in my heart, I wish them no harm.

To live in harmony with the things that we don't like is truly a blessing, for ourselves, the planet and all other beings. It is not necessary to kill or destroy that which we don't like.

When we act from purity, the need to defend or explain our actions does not arise. If there is no self, no ego performing, who is there to explain anything?

It is the ego, the delusion that we are someone and something that always needs to be defended and that can always justify and explain every deed we perform.
It is the ego that needs to be accepted by others, praised and given a 'pat on the back'. When this aspect of us acts, it is always with an ulterior motive. Self-promotion.

Now try this experiment for a week. Don't defend yourself. If you do something wrong, apologise and let it go. Don't attempt to justify or explain it. Don't demand that others see your point of view or understand you. Just let it go. Don't feed the ego!

When Ananda, the Buddha's cousin and attendant for twenty five years, was wrongly accused of misconduct, he simply answered his accusers by saying, 'In my heart I did no wrong, but if you say I did, I apologise'.

No explanation, no justification, no defence. Only an answer coming from the purity of being.

And if you perform an act of kindness, stay quiet. Again, there is no need to explain why you did what you did. It is done, gone, finished. Let it go.

The purpose of spiritual training is to assist the forces of ego and conceit to die out, and to allow the pure mind to manifest. This mind simply is. When this mind is present, where are you? Where is ego?
Pure mind and ego are like light and darkness. They cannot exist in the same place in the same moment. When the pure mind is not present, there you are with all your views, opinions beliefs and conceit. A bundle of delusion, making its way in the world, causing chaos for all concerned.

Every moment we are awake is a moment to be. A moment to let this pure mind manifest by not allowing the influences of ego and self-preservation come to the fore. When the mind pulls in the direction of ego, simply see it for what it is and let it go.
You are not your mind, and you are not your body.
There is nothing that you really are, and no mould that you have to fit. Be yourself. Act from a position of egolessness. Set yourself free.

I am turning on the light – where does the darkness go?

Looking at ourselves
'What place can hide us from ourselves?'

After a famous meditation teacher had passed away, a blind man who lived close to the monastery told a friend, "Since I am blind, I cannot watch a person's face, so I must judge his character by the sound of his voice. Usually when I hear someone congratulate another upon his happiness or success, I also hear a secret tone of envy or jealousy. Also, when I hear condolence for the misfortune of another, I hear pleasure or a faint trace of satisfaction in that person's voice. However in all my experience with the Master, his voice was always sincere. Whenever he expressed happiness, I heard nothing but happiness. When he expressed sorrow, sorrow was all I heard."

At the very heart of spiritual practice is meditation, the turning away from the world of ego and the senses, and the investigation of mind and body. The foundation of who and what we think we are. This investigation can continue for many lifetimes as the layers of ego and conceit are slowly eroded and our true nature revealed. The method of meditation we use in this investigation is insight meditation (Vipassana Bhavana). It is the only way to truly see and know ourselves as we really are.

In this form of meditation, nothing is hidden, for the very object or attention is only our own mind and body. What place can hide us from ourselves?

All our fears, doubts, desires and delusions are revealed in an atmosphere of calm and balanced observation. Eventually, nothing will escape the detached watchfulness. But to do this we need to be brave. We need to go deep into the heart of a powerful delusion as to who and what we think we are.

No matter how honest we believe ourselves to be, our usual everyday mind has created an image that is untrue.

We may think that we are kind and generous people, always willing to help others and to be of service but the reality is often something other than that.
Conversely, we may believe that we are low and unworthy, not good enough for the trust and friendship of others, but this too is not true.
Whatever view we hold about ourselves is just a view. It is not the truth.

Because of our basic delusion as to how we regard ourselves, we all suffer from the same condition, that of ego. The part of us which believes itself to be real and lasting. To be a definite force on the world, for better or worse. It is this part that holds all its own views and opinions, and of course always believes itself to be the best.

It is this part that does not want to die or to be eradicated, and solely for this reason, can be very devious. It knows every level of subtlety and deceit. It can fool others but more importantly, it can fool us. This ego has been around for a very long time gathering strength and vitality always waiting for an opportunity to assert itself.

We believe that we were something in the past, and that we will be something in the future. When ego arises, a history arises, and when that history arises the whole delusion of who and what we are arises.

Without investigation, attachment to ego will never be broken. We will never be free from its influence, and the unhappiness it inevitably brings.

This ego is always out for itself. It is always after a prize, a reward, sometimes large sometimes small, but always something. Perhaps it is something as subtle as simply feeling good after performing a kindness or just needing a 'thank you' for a gift or work done, but whatever it is, it always needs and demands something for itself from every situation.

Always.

Generally speaking, we like to think of ourselves in a favourable light. A person of integrity and substance. Someone worthy of the respect and approval of others. In short, an all-round nice person. Even when we do perform an unwholesome act and suffer the pricks of conscience, we can usually justify our action and put it behind is.

Onward, onward to the future, carrying all our past habits conditioning with us. Because of ego (self identity) we are always self-centred and self-motivated. Before spiritual awakening this is how it is for all of us.

Ego is the manifestation of ignorance.

Insight meditation (Vipassana Bhavana) is not only the

investigation of this process, but also the breaking of it.

By recognising ego as the cause of our unhappiness, we can make a decision not to feed it any more. Not to indulge its fantasies, and so take away its power.

The Buddha has said that the best way to put out a fire is to simply not add any more fuel to it. To let it burn itself out. Ego is the fire within us.

However, once we begin this process of no longer feeding the ego, we have to allow the stockpile of conceit and confusion accumulated in the past to rise up from the deeper realms of the mind, and let them go. Let everything go.

We have to give up any views of who and what we think we are and be open to whatever arises. This means to no longer identify ourselves as a particular type of person who should think or act in a certain way. These views are just conditioning, indoctrinated into us by our parents, friends, peers and the rest of society in general.

In reality there are no set patterns that we have to adhere to.

To think that we should never have cruel or unkind thoughts will only create problems for us, because when we lift the lid off this dustbin of our mind, to be sure they will be there.

Our habits and conditioning arise from the past to confront us now in the present. They are inescapable. In order not to empower these thoughts for the future we have to see them for what they really are, mental states arising because of conditions. Not 'me', not 'mine', not what 'I am'.

This mind stream flows on and on, every thought experienced and acted upon in this moment affecting it and conditioning it for the future. This is the process we have to break.

In the end, ego is not a problem. To think of ourselves as good, or to think of ourselves as bad or unworthy, is merely the opportunity to train. To see ourselves as we really are. Simply a mass of ever-changing moods, thoughts, feelings and emotions affecting the accumulation of matter we call the body. Nothing more than that.
There is no underlying 'self' that we really are. No cosmic 'soul' or entity that is in any way worthy of praise or blame. Just process. The whole of our existence is just process. An activity of becoming that never becomes anything.

This is what we have to investigate.

The ego is without substance. The 'self' or 'soul' is without substance. Nothing was ever born and nothing will ever die, but as long as we are attached to mind and body, the delusion of self, it will always appear that way.

Insight meditation (Vipassana Bhavana) only investigates this delusion. The delusion of self. It doesn't say it is real, and it doesn't say it is not real. It says, 'look for your self, what you see?'
Pleasant thoughts arise by themselves, so do the unpleasant ones. Nothing lasts for more than a moment and everything is a part of this changing process.

Give up your identification with your habitual thought patterns see what you really are and what you really are not.

You're not the body, and you're not the mind.

Be free.

Love openly
'When we know where to look for the truth
our problems and judgements fall away.'

There was once a nun who went to train at an exclusively male monastery.
She was very disciplined in her practice and also very beautiful. Because of this, many of the monks quickly fell in love with her. One monk was so overwhelmed by her beauty that he could not resist writing her a note.
The note said, 'I love you very much, meet me in the garden after evening meditation'.
As she walked past him one day whilst entering the meditation hall, he handed it to her. When the meditation had finished, she read the note and stood up. Facing a monk who had written it, she said, 'if you truly love me so much come here and embrace me now'.
The monk hung his head in shame.

In Dhamma terms we say, 'If you love, love openly'.
This simply means to be honest with our feelings and motivations. To be sincere. To have integrity in the world. This is not usually how we live. So many games being played, so many people looking for their own share of happiness, so much confusion and so much pain.

Everyone wants to be happy, of course, and for most of us this includes an intimate relationship with another person. Someone we can share our life with. Someone we can grow with. Someone we can love. However, our expectations of our partner can be very high indeed and often the feeling arises that they have failed is in some way. Perhaps they are irritable in the mornings, or they don't want help around the house. Maybe they are just not good at dealing with the finances, but often our response is to believe that they have let us down in some way and we feel that the one person we had pinned all our hopes of happiness on to is in fact, not the one for us. Perhaps we need to find someone else. Someone else who can make us happy.

One young woman I know asked me if I knew of any way to make her boyfriend jealous. When I asked why she would want to do such a thing she replied, 'Because I want him to marry me'.
This is a very dangerous game to play, and one would have to question her motivation. In any case, it would seem unlikely that this relationship could be happy in the long term if it was established on such an unwholesome mental state as jealousy.

It is true that when we don't know the nature of our mind we don't look at the outcome of what we do. Because of our confusion we create certain monsters and set them free. We hope for the best, but they always come back to hurt us. Always.

To love openly means to be free from self-centred motivation and to give love. To be accepting of other people and respect them. Even if they are doing things that we think they should not do. Even if they behave in a way we don't approve of. Even if they hurt us.

In worldly relationships, we always work on the other person trying to mould them to suit ourselves. In a Dhamma relationship, we work on ourselves. Checking our motivation and looking at the results of our action. If our motivation is pure whatever happens as the outcome, we are blameless. We don't have to make excuses and we don't have to find someone else to blame either.

A Dhamma life means a pure life. It is a gradual growth from ego to egolessness. A movement from darkness to light. Along this path, there will be many problems and difficulties, but if we keep our motivation pure, the outcome will always be beneficial.

When we no longer live in the world acting upon our selfish desires and habits we demonstrate love. It's truly that simple.

Love is not something we need to cultivate and develop. It is a quality we already have. When we don't have an ego based self directing everything we do, love manifests.

This is to love openly. Not in secret, not with shame, not with an ulterior emotive, or the fear that someone may find out exactly what we are doing, but with an openness established in pure motivation.

It is the practice of letting go.

When we judge others and complain about their actions, we are always looking outside ourselves. We are missing the point of Vipassana and insight training.

Insight training means to look at the mind that is actually

making those judgements and not the object of them. It means to have a clear picture of what is really happening, and where it is happening. Not outside. Not in the world. But in our own mind. Only in our mind. When we know where to look for the truth, all our problems and judgements fall away.

One meditation Master has said, 'No one ever became wise through criticising others'.

Wisdom only arises when we look at ourselves, at the ego and its selfish desire for personal happiness. Now we can see that thoughts, moods, feelings and emotions are like clouds passing through a clear sky, and to each one we can say, 'this is not me, this is not mine, this is not what I am.'

The qualities we think we want, such as kindness, compassion, tolerance and love are already well established in the heart. Be what you really are. Don't let ego get in the way. Life is too precious for that.

So in your life be happy. In your meditation go deep, and in your love, give it freely. Love openly and without conditions. Love is too beautiful, too valuable to be a part of the barter system of life. It is something that we need to give freely and without expectation of something in return. I will love you if you love me back, is not love. It is a trade. It is a businessman's love. It cannot ever be beautiful and so cannot ever be sustained. It is only a game.

Let your need for love be overwhelmed by your desireless desire to give love. Let your spiritual heart transform the emotional heart, and let your pain and suffering fall away into the emptiness of the universe.

Keep it simple
'Spiritual life is essentially a simple affair.'

There was once a Master called Kitano Gempo. The whole of his training was devoted to the breaking of attachment. When he was twenty years old and living as a wandering mendicant, he met a fellow traveller who smoked tobacco. As they rested one day, the traveller offered a smoke to Kitano, which he accepted as he was very hungry at the time. Kitano enjoyed this smoke and when he and the traveller parted, he was given the gift of a pipe and some tobacco. Soon however, he realised how attached he was becoming to smoking, so he gave it up.
'This tobacco is very pleasant, and such pleasant things may disturb my meditation,' he thought.
Later in life, he found himself having to endure a cold and hard winter. He wrote a letter to his Master, asking for some warm clothes. They never arrived. Knowing that his Master would not deliberately ignore his plight, he decided to find out whether his letter had been received or not. To do this he consulted the I Ching, the ancient Chinese book of divination . The results could not be disputed. The letter had not been received. This fact was later confirmed by a message from his Master, making no mention of his request for warm clothes. 'If I perform such accurate work with the I Ching, I may neglect my meditation,' thought Kitano, and so he gave it up. He never consulted it again. As he grew older he studied Chinese calligraphy and

poetry. He became so skilful in this art that even his teachers praised him. Once again Kitano saw these merely as distractions to his meditation. 'If I don't stop now, I will become a poet, not a Master of Dhamma', he thought, and so immediately stopped.

He never wrote another poem again.

Spiritual life is essentially a simple affair. To progress in it means to watch our attachments fall away until we are left with the purity of being.

Selflessness.

Ordinary life is just the opposite. Holding onto more and more things. Material objects, favourite possessions, memories, opinions and ideas. Identification with our mind and body. To realise our spiritual potential we must break our attachments. We must give up clinging.

However this may sound, it doesn't actually mean we have to give everything away or no longer hold any views or opinions, it means we have to break our attachment to them. We have to see them for what they are.

Often we hear it said that 'Money is the root of all evil'. But this is not correct. The correct expression is, 'The love of money is the root of all evil'.

Money is fine. Money itself is completely neutral. It is our love of money or our attachment to it that causes all the problems.

Money, people, life is never the problem. Attachment is the problem.

At one time the Buddha was sitting with King Bimbisara.

The King, who was already a lay disciple and prominent supporter of the Buddha, asked a question.

"Master, in the world there seems to be so much suffering and pain, but I would like to know where suffering and pain really begin?"

"Your majesty, all suffering and all pain begins with love and attachment."

The king could not accept this answer and so, in front of the Buddha and without reflection, he rejected this reply.

"No, no, no, this cannot be true, there must be something else, something you are not telling me. I ask you again, please tell me truly, where does suffering and pain really begin?"

"Your majesty," answered the Buddha, "I tell you truly that all suffering and all pain begins with love and attachment."

For the second time this answer was rejected and the question was asked again. The Buddha, speaking only from truth and wisdom, replied for the third time in the same way.

At this point the king relaxed, and letting go of his resistance to the truth, and his fixed views of life asked the Buddha to explain his answer.

"Your majesty," began the Buddha, "imagine that your son was kidnapped by bandits and held to ransom. These bandits threatened to torture horribly your son, and eventually kill him if the ransom was not met. Now, I ask you to tell me, how you think you would feel?"

"This would be something terrible for me," said the king, "a tremendous suffering in my life and a tremendous pain in my heart. I cannot imagine anything more horrible. Naturally I would comply completely with the demands of the bandits and do anything for the safe and speedy return of my son."

"Now, your majesty," continued the Buddha, "imagine the same situation with someone else, not your son but the son of a neighbouring king. In this instance, how do you think you would feel?"

"Well," began the king, "the situation is still horrible of course, but naturally for me it would not be the same, and I would not suffer or feel pain in my heart as I would for my own son."

"So you see your majesty," concluded the Buddha, "the cause behind all of the suffering and pain that we meet in our life, is only our love and attachment for people and things. Without this attachment there can be no suffering."

We tend to complicate our lives, because we can't let go. We prescribe certain rules for particular people and objects, the ones we are close to and not for others. For those we don't care so much.

If you lose your expensive watch my concern will not be a strong as if I had lost my watch. I might even call you careless and stupid, but the circumstances surrounding the loss of my watch I would call something else. An accident, and possibly not even my fault, and I would definitely suffer more.

Attachment and clinging.

To really progress along the spiritual path, we need to simplify our life. We need to develop an honest foundation. Honesty with ourselves and our motivations and from that, honesty with all beings. This we can only do by purifying our centre, our spiritual heart.

If we are to speak we should keep our language simple. Say what we mean and mean what we say. There is no need to enter into a long intellectual discussion reinforcing our own particular point of view. Just say what has to be said and let it go.

And don't look for results either. From a pure centre, we can always say what we feel without anticipating a response.

The simplicity and economy of words became very apparent to me one time during a boat journey from Folkestone to the Hook of Holland.

I was sitting next to a young man from Morocco. We had exchanged a few words with each ther, but his English wasn't too good. He stood up, intending to go to the cafeteria, and asked me if I would like a drink.

"Oh yes. That will be really nice. It's very kind of you. If you are sure it is not too much trouble. I can always go myself. I don't want to put you out. Okay, I have a tea please." I said.

He looked at me and walked away. When he returned he had brought only one drink with him. The one for himself. I realised immediately that I had said too much and he had not understood. Instead of simply asking for a cup of tea, I had spoken for too long and only managed to confuse him.

Say what you mean and keep it simple.

The clearest way of expressing this attitude of simplicity and honesty is with the expression, 'Always face the Dhamma'.

Dhamma is a Buddhist word that means ultimate truth.

When our intention is always to live life by facing the ultimate truth, what can go wrong? Even when things don't go according to our plans, we can always be open to their teaching.

If we don't look for happiness, happiness comes by itself.

However, we need to be open and not attach ourselves to our fantasies and endless mental projections.
It is said that in the mind of the true spiritual practitioner, there are no desires, only preferences.
This means to let go of the attachment towards our own ideas of how things should be for us and accept everything as it is. If you have the desire to sleep in a comfortable bed but the only thing available is the settee, you will be unhappy. However, if you only have a preference for a comfortable bed, when the settee is offered you will accept it graciously.
Not only that, you will not hold in your mind, the attraction of a bed. This is real happiness. Accepting the conditions you cannot change and being at peace with them.

Trying to sleep on a settee whilst wishing you were in a nice comfortable bed is just more suffering!

It is true that when we first become involved in a spiritual practice there seems to be so many things about ourselves, we need to change. Our fear, our greed, our jealousy. So many different things wrong with us that the task is endless. But the teaching here is to keep it simple. There is no need to change everything in our life. We just need to change one thing from that, everything else flows.

By itself, with no effort involved.

But what is that one thing?

It is our heart. Our spiritual heart.

Let go of ego. Let go of trying to control the world and make everything perfect for you and simply be open. Work with what you have. It is not possible to make everything right all the time, no matter how hard you try. Understand that and turn inward.
The spiritual life is not a secret. Its truths are all around us. No need to change anything. Just be. From that, everything changes anyway.

So how do we learn to let go of all things, we are attached to?

Think about it. How do we let go of anything?

We simply relax our grip and let them fall away. No effort is required. Effort is only needed to hold onto them. All the pain, heartache and disappointment in life is caused by holding onto things that are already, by their very nature, moving away from us.
Through not letting go.

Keep it simple. Keep everything simple.
Simplify your life by letting go of the things that hurt you. Recognise that life itself, however it manifests, is the opportunity to allow all the pain and suffering you experience just by being alive, to fall away.

The teachings of the greatest Masters can always be explained simply. Follow their example, let go of what you are attached to and discover real and lasting happiness. The happiness of liberation.

The empty mind
'There is only one mind.'

There were once two Masters of opposite characteristics. One kept the Buddhist precepts scrupulously and so never drank alcohol or ate in the afternoon, whilst the other often enjoyed a drink and ate whenever he felt like it.

One day the first Master visited the second one, who was drinking a glass of sake.

"Hello Brother," said the second Master, "will you have a drink?"

"I never drink," said the first Master solemnly.

"One who does not drink is not even human," replied the second Master.

"You mean to call me inhuman," exclaimed the first Master, "just because I will not drink alcohol? If I am not a human, then please tell me exactly what I am."

"A Buddha," replied the second Master.

Often, when we embark upon a spiritual lifestyle we hold very high expectations of ourselves. We listen to beautiful Dhamma talks about the refined qualities of mind, such as love, compassion and joy, sometimes even experiencing them directly for ourselves. We begin to feel that this is how things should always be for us. Calm, peaceful and loving. Living in harmony with all things.

And then something happens!

The situation occurs and we feel we've lost it.

Gone are those calm and peaceful feelings we treasured so much and what is left is anger, resentment and even hatred. But that is not all. Also arising with these feelings is the thought, 'I shouldn't feel like this'. Now those feelings become compounded.

At first there was just anger, but now there is anger and guilt. Then remorse. Then the desire to feel different. Then the wish that the incident had never happened and the sense of failure in practice. On and on it goes. Round and round. Spinning wildly in confusion and totally out of control.

In the book Inner Chapters, Chuang Tsu tells us that, No Self is True Self.

This is a very beautiful way of expressing that which cannot be expressed. The truth of our reality. That behind every movement of mind, there is nothing. Only emptiness.

No-Self.

Only a delusive attachment to our mental states as being who and what we are. When these mental states are noble and worthy, we feel happy, we feel we are expressing our true nature, our true self. However, when these mental states are low and unworthy, we feel a sense of guilt and shame, believing these to come from a darker side. Our enemy within.

We fail to see that they all begin in the same place.

The mind.

There is only one mind. Not many.

Not the mind we want, and the mind we don't want. Not the mind we face in meditation, and the mind we take back into the world with us. Not the mind we love with and the mind we hate with. Only one mind with each thought, mood, feeling and emotion emanating from the same place.

And all these thoughts, moods, feelings and emotions have the same quality. Whether they are pleasant or unpleasant, noble or low, they are all simply passing through the consciousness, like sticks floating down a river, or like clouds passing through an empty sky.
Behind every passing moment of anger or resentment, hostility or hatred, is the empty mind. The mind of No-Self, the Pure Mind.

So what to do?
The answer is always simple.
Let go. Just let go.

If anger arises, let it go. If guilt about the anger arises, let that go too. Let everything go until the purity of No-Self shines through.

A student once asked his Master, "If there is nothing in my mind, what should I do?"
The Master replied, "Throw it out."
"But," the student continued, "if I haven't anything in my mind, how can I throw it out?"
"Very well then," said the Master, " carry it out!"

Whatever arises into the mind, let it go. It's not you anyway so why hold onto it?

It is the very holding on to all the things that we think are ourselves that causes all our pain and suffering.
Anger is not what we are. Guilt is not what we are. Resentment is not what we are. Happiness is not what we are. These qualities are simply movements of mind arising because of conditions. Once we recognise them for what they truly are, we can let them go. Now they have no power over us. The more we let go, the more peaceful our lives become.

One great meditation master has said:

> 'Let go a little and there is a little peace.
> Let go a lot, and there is a lot of peace.
> Let go completely and there is complete peace'.

Complete peace arising from an empty mind. A mind free from the attachment and delusion that these things are what we are.

In truth, there is nothing that we really are, and no way we have to be.
Make 'letting go' your life, until there is no more to let go of.

Be free.

Living in the sunshine
'People are the way they are, that is their choice.
You are the way you are, that is your choice.'

A feudal lord once asked a Master of Dhamma, how he might pass the time. He felt his days to be very long, attending to his office and sitting stiffly to receive the homage of others. The Master wrote eight Chinese characters on a piece of paper and gave them to the lord. The characters read:
> This day will not come again,
> each minute is worth a priceless gem.

There are only two ways to live, the right way and the wrong way. This is the choice that faces all of us. How do you want to live?

The wrong way is the most popular choice.
Seeing life as a series of problems to be resolved, as a struggle against all the misfortunes that can befall a person. Creating an ideal scenario in our mind of how things should be, a mental utopia and then working as hard as possible to make it a reality for us.
We carry memories from the past and then compare our present and future to them. 'Was I happier then?' 'Will I be happy again?'
We continually repeat the same formulas for personal happiness and when they fail to fully satisfy us, we simply

start again. Mistakes made in the past are repeated over and over and our quest is always the same. Personal happiness, a sense of well-being and a pleasant life. We fall into the trap of believing, 'if only I had that I would be happy'. Or, 'if only I didn't have that I would be happy'. Happiness is always seen as the goal of the future, something that we have to work towards. I am not happy now, but in ten years if all goes well, I will be.

Because of this very projection we miss the moment. We miss the possibility of now.

In reality there is no time other than now. The past is just a memory and the future is just an idea. And when do we experience the past and future? Now, right now, in this very moment and at no other time.

Every memory that arises is experienced as a thought, now. Every future plan that arises is experienced as a thought, now. There is no time other than now. Everything else is imagination.

When I first began teaching in India, in the small town of Budh Gaya, the place of the Buddha's enlightenment, I would often visit the stupa that marks this important event, early in the morning.

My reason for doing this as, with most visitors to the area, was to perform Kora, or circumambulation of the shrine. This is to walk in meditation around the main object of veneration, the Bodhi tree, and the surrounding area.

Because the stupa, which is something like a small religious park, is surrounded by a wall, the rising sun shines directly onto one part, and only partially on the other. I noticed that each time I reached the shaded area, I would cross over into the sunshine again, and therefore perform the whole of my Kora, taking about one hour, enjoying the light and warmth of the sun.

It is no secret that the sun has a pleasant effect upon us and generally makes everyone feel better. It's the winter we dread, never the summer. For most people the summer cannot come quickly enough, and usually passes too soon. For me in Budh Gaya, to come out of the shade into the sunshine was a natural response. I did it without thinking. It was a spontaneous action.

As I continued my walking meditation, I began to reflect upon this action. Of course, there was no need to move out of the shade and into the sunlight. I could have easily kept walking without any noticeable discomfort, but the choice was natural. It wasn't something I had to think about.

As my reflection or contemplation continued, a compassion arose within me and I began to realise that most people live their lives struggling in the shadows. Trapped in the cold and the dark. Always wanting things to be different, but not knowing how to make significant and lasting changes. Not knowing how to move into the sunlight.

The sunlight of course, represents a relaxed and easy approach to life. A harmonious attitude to all things, a sense of joy at being alive and a peaceful acceptance of everything as it is. The shadows however, represent the opposite aspects. Difficulties, isolation, separateness from the rest of existence, and a sense of struggle.

In short, the right way and the wrong way to live.

It is within our power to come out of the shadows and walk in the sunlight. It only involves a crossing over. Just one step. Happiness, joy and an appreciation of life are qualities we can all experience, because they are not qualities we have to create. They wait silently and patiently for their liberation in our heart. It only requires a change in attitude. To no longer see life as a constant battle, always struggling to control everyone and everything around us so that we can be happy. To be in the sunlight means to relax and be open, allowing everything to be as it is. Good or bad. Pleasant or unpleasant. People are the way they are, that is their choice. You are the way you are, that is your choice. How do you choose to live, in the sunshine or in the shade?

Each moment that passes becomes a memory, and this present moment will never come again. Once experienced it is gone forever. Life is such a precious gift that to drift through it as though asleep is to completely waste the wonderful opportunity we have. No-one can say how difficult it is to take birth as a human being but once we have it, not to use it to its fullest potential is to miss an opportunity that will never come again.

Give yourself to the practice of awareness. Make it the most important thing in your life. Become a witness to your mind and body. Know your own reality.
There is nothing else you need to do. Study is unnecessary, becoming involved in a new and exotic religion is unnecessary and trying to understand how the universe operates is also unnecessary. Just keep watching yourself. Calmly, dispassionately and lovingly and everything will

be revealed. Eventually, everything will be revealed.

The Sun is always shining.
Even when we can't see it or feel it's warmth, it's there. It never goes away. It doesn't rise and set at all, that is only the appearance of it. Without investigation that's how it looks, but we all know that it is the earth's movement around the sun that causes this illusion.
It's how it looks, but is not the truth.

Don't be fooled by appearances. Go beyond how things seem to be. Come into the sunshine and find the right way to live.

No-one can do it for you
'In meditation, we face ourselves'

There was once a Japanese wrestler who was immensely strong and talented. In private bouts he defeated even his own teacher. However in public, it was a different matter. Even the most inexperienced of opponents could defeat him easily. Naturally he was very concerned by this and so he sought the help of a Dhamma Master.

"You are called O Nami, which means Great Waves," said the Dhamma Master, "so tonight I want you to stay in this temple and meditate. Imagine you are those sweeping billows. You are no longer a wrestler who was afraid, but you are instead those huge waves washing away everything before you. Do this and you will become the greatest wrestler in the land."

O Nami did as he was asked. As the night progressed, he imagined himself first as ripples, and then increasing his power and becoming bigger and stronger. In his mind he was washing away everything in sight. Even the statue of the Buddha was not safe from his mighty force.

In the morning the Dhamma Master returned to find O Nami still deep in meditation, but now with a faint smile on his face.

He patted the wrestlers shoulder and said, "Now nothing can disturb you. You are those great waves that you were named after. You will sweep away everything before you."

The same day O Nami entered a new wrestling contest and

won. After that no one was able to defeat him.

Meditation is a powerful force in our lives. With it we can change everything about the way we live. However, like O Nami in the story, even with the help of a Dhamma Master, the work that had to be done, he had to do by himself.
Even with expert guidance he was alone. In the end it was only him and his mind.

There are many stories of gurus, dynamic and powerful teachers who with only a touch or a magic formula, are able to enlighten others. Spiritual seekers often impressed by such stories and will expend a great deal of time and effort locating a teacher with this kind of reputation, just to be touched by them and spend time in their presence. However, whatever they may believe happens in such contact, what definitely does not happen is the eradication of their delusion and ignorance. This cannot be done by another. It has to be done by ourselves.

The Buddha taught for forty five years after his enlightenment. It was his wish that as many people as possible would benefit from his teaching and so attain their own liberation. He would have liked to have ended all the suffering in the world and see everyone as him, perfectly free.
If he could have done this simply by embracing someone or touching their head, to be sure, he would have done it.

However, the Buddha said:

> Purity and impurity are personal concerns.
> No one can purify another.
>
> Dhammapada: verse 165

Meditation is the key to self purity and to liberation. There is no difference between the two. Once we have removed greed, hatred and delusion from the mind, we are already free. We don't have to wait until we are dead. We can do it now.

Of course, in spiritual training, we need a teacher, someone who has already walked this path and can show us the way by explaining to us the simplicity of practice. However, this is all they can do. Point, instruct and possibly even bully us into practice, but they cannot do the practice for us. This is the one thing we have to do for ourselves.

At one time, a disciple asked his Master, if he would accompany him on a long and difficult journey.

The Master replied, "Of course, I will go with you if you ask, but I can't help you very much. If you are hungry, I cannot eat for you, if you are thirsty I cannot drink for you and if you need to go to the toilet, I cannot go for you."

When the disciple heard these words, he was enlightened.

In meditation we face ourselves. We face our past. All our memories and conditioning rise up to confront us and we have to sit quietly and let them pass. Painful or pleasant, good or bad, we have to let them go. This activity we have to do alone. Once in meditation, we are by ourselves, facing ourselves. This is why we need to be brave and prepared to go deep. To penetrate all the delusions we hold about ourselves and the world.

Many non-meditators think of meditation as an escape from the world, of settling back into a quiet and peaceful environment and giving up in real life. Nothing could be further from the truth. Meditation is a true facing of the world. Our world. The one that we create with our thoughts, moods, feelings and emotions and the one we most definitely live in.

In meditation we don't look at others and we don't follow someone else's breathing pattern. We turn to our own breath and allow everything else to fall away.

Even in a meditation hall filled with people, we are always alone. In good company possibly, but always alone.

This is such a beautiful practice and is ultimately the only thing that will lead to insight and enlightenment. This practice of awareness.

We take this attitude of careful watching, of witnessing our own mind and its habitual reactions into our everyday life with us, not confining it to formal meditation practice only, but applying it to all situations. We are alone in meditation and we are alone in life. There is just us, responsible for all the pain and unhappiness that we experience.

No-one is to blame. We do it to ourselves.

Many people complain that after the initial blissful experiences of a newly begun awareness practice, their meditation becomes busy and confused, as they are bombarded by thoughts and feelings that are completely unexpected. Gone is the peace of those earlier sittings and now arising is the desire to return to the way it used to be.

However contrary it may seem, in actual fact, this is a good sign. The past being released into the present, that we can face without our usual habits of suppression or indulgence. This we call the Process of Purification.

It is like the story of the man who wanted to leave the town he had always lived in.
This particular man had grown up in his home town. He had married, raised a family and gone into business. In order to do this he had borrowed a lot of money.
One day, the man decided to leave the town behind him and begin a new life elsewhere. However, before he could do this he had to pay back all his debts. Everything he had borrowed in the past had to be repaid.

This is exactly how it is for us in our meditation. Repaying all our debts of the past. No-one can do this for us. They are our debts and only we can repay them. Personally.
This is the ultimate teaching in spiritual practice. We are always by ourselves, reaping the results of the past.

There are many gurus in the world with a great many powers, but in truth the greatest power belongs to us. The ability to let our past go and be completely free from its influence.

This is how the greatest Masters teach. Showing us that our development is within our own hands only. No-one can do it for us. Only we can set ourselves free.

Don't miss this opportunity. The moment to change our life is right here, right now.

Only you can do it!

Higher than happiness
'There is a way to live that is in fact, higher than happiness.'

At one time Daiju visited the master Baso in China.
Baso asked, "What do you seek?"
"Enlightenment," replied Daiju.
"You have your own treasure house, why do you seek outside?" asked Baso.
Daiju inquired, "Where is my treasure house?"
Baso answered, "What you're asking for is contained within your own treasure house."
Daiju was enlightened. From then on he urged his own disciples to open their own treasure house and use those treasures.

As human beings our goal is the same. It doesn't matter if we are Easterners or Westerners, highly intelligent and sophisticated or completely stupid. It doesn't matter where we live either. In a village in the Brazilian jungle or in a modern city in the so-called first world. We all want the same. We want to be happy.

Actually, this is not such an unreasonable request, is it?
We are born into this world and at some point, usually quite early, experience unhappiness and we don't like it. It doesn't feel good. Perhaps just as a baby when we are too hot or too cold, or we want feeding or changing, we experience feelings of discomfort, and we react. We want

to change our present situation for something much more favourable. As we grow and develop mentally we become more and more subtle as to our demands.

We hold the concept of happiness within us, and then try to arrange everything contained in our sphere of control to promote the concept. Perhaps now we don't simply cry out for conditions to change as we did when we were babies, but apart from that everything is the same. We know what we want and if we don't get it we suffer.

Happiness is very elusive. It comes and goes by itself. There is nothing any of us can do with any certainty to determine its arising and nothing we can do to make it stay once it appears. This is the nature of happiness. It comes and goes due to conditions. It is completely impersonal.

Of course, happiness is real.

We can say it's vague and difficult to define, but we all know what it feels like. It feels pleasant, and that's what we want. A life filled with only pleasant feelings. No one enjoys the opposite of happiness. Depression, frustration, irritation, stress, doubt and all the rest. These are the feelings we try to keep away. It is a constant battle each day. The feelings we want contrasted to the feelings that we don't want.

So how do we attempt to promote the feelings we want?
By turning outwards into the material, emotional and spiritual world. By organising the different aspects of life, so that we are never unhappy.

Of course, it doesn't work does it?

Each time we acquire a new material possession we feel happy. The new iphone, or washing machine, or car, or house, or anything at all we experience a happy feeling. In this sense, happiness is real. However, this feeling of happiness doesn't last. It has no sustaining power. Soon it passes and although we may have a new material possession in our life, it just becomes one more thing to worry about, or keep in good repair, or simply carry around with us. In reality, it just becomes a burden.

In the emotional life we need people to love and care for us so that we can be happy. How often have we met the man or woman of our dreams, only to find that they fail us in some way? They are not the people who can make us happy all the time.

Families are the same. Our parents, children, brothers and sisters, fail to meet our expectations of them and again we suffer. We feel let down and disappointed. Our hopes for happiness through them dashed.

The spiritual life is no different. By turning outwards to a new religion or system of living, we feel we can be happy. Initially, as with the material and the emotional world this can be true, but unless we investigate the inherent nature of happiness and unhappiness, this too will fail us.

The new religion can be like a new car. At first, it brings happiness, but then, when things begin to go wrong, it just becomes another burden. Perhaps then we feel that changes in order and so we look for something else. Something that will bring back that feeling of happiness.

Actually, happiness is not the problem.

It is our attachment to it that creates our suffering and dissatisfaction.
It is time now to turn away from looking outside ourselves for happiness and understand where happiness truly begins and ends.

The Buddha understood this clearly when he was living as a Prince, in his father's palace. Even though he had and could have anything he wanted, he was still not happy all the time. He would be faced with boredom, frustration and disappointment and the whole range of human emotions, just like the poorest beggars outside the palace walls.
Even when we have everything we think we need for happiness, we still cannot determine its arising.

So what can we do?

There is a way we can live that is in fact, higher than happiness.

Through the practice of Insight Meditation (Vipassana Bhavana), we can examine the very source of our unhappiness and the desire to change the situation we find ourselves in. Through the constant determination of recognising all of our thoughts, moods, feelings and emotions as not 'me', not 'mine', not what 'I am', we release ourselves from their grasp.

This is not magic. This is not a special technique available to adherents of only a certain religion. This is the potential

for human beings. To understand the mind and body as they truly are. Not 'me', not 'mine', and not what 'I am'.
As this understanding begins to grow through the cultivation of our practice of meditation, the simplistic desire for happiness and the insistence that everyone and everything conduct themselves according to our small and highly limited view so that we may experience that happiness, falls away. By no longer trying to control the universe to suit our particular demands, but beautifully and lovingly allowing everything to 'be', we experience peace.

No more struggle. No more fight. No more suffering.
Surrendering it into this state we experience the mind that is, indeed, higher than happiness. We benefit from this beautiful internal peace and spaciousness, and so ultimately all beings benefit.
We no longer add to the general confusion of the world as just one more ego simply wanting its own way, but we abide patiently, knowing when to speak and when to keep quiet. When to act and went to be still.

This is such a wonderful practice. The way of effortless effort. Of knowing things as they really are, and living in harmony with that truth.

The Japanese Zen Buddhists say this very beautifully in the verse:

> Sitting quietly doing nothing,
> spring comes
> and the grass grows by itself.

Sitting quietly doing nothing, is the meditation practice. Not trying to control the mind but being at peace with it. The pleasant and the unpleasant. The interesting and the boring. The peaceful and the exciting. Realising that all our thoughts, moods, feelings and emotions come and go without end. If this is their nature, why try to hold on to some at the expense of others?
Let them go. Let them all go.

Spring comes, is the result of this practice. The peace and understanding that arises from it. It is the fruit of our effort. The ability to enjoy without grasping, the pleasant moments of mind, and to be peaceful and patient with the unpleasant moments.

And the grass grows by itself, is the effect this practice has in our lives. Not confining itself to formal meditation sittings, but radiating outwards from our heart to influence and affect the way we live in the world. Moment after moment.

There is nothing extra you need to do. There is nowhere you need to be. Everything is right here for you right now. Turn to yourself and begin to experience a way of living that is beyond the selfish and ultimately immature demands to be happy, and realise a life that is indeed, higher than happiness.

Muddy Road
'We are always striving
to create the perfect conditions for happiness.'

At one time two monks were travelling together along a wet and muddy road. Rounding a bend they met a beautiful young women in a silk kimono and sash, unable to cross the intersection.

One monk recognised her need and immediately swept her up in his arms and carried her through the mud. The other monk followed silently and did not speak for the rest of the day. Finally they reached the monastery where they would stay for the night, but in this moment the second monk could no longer restrain himself.

"We monks," he cried, "are not even supposed to look at young and beautiful women, but you actually picked one up and carried her. Why did you do that?"

"I left that young woman standing by the side of the road," said the first monk, "do you still carry her?"

It is sure that many people carry the pains of slights and insults from the past with them today. Somebody, perhaps many years ago, hurt them and instead of leaving it where it belongs, in the past, they carry it with them throughout their life, allowing it to influence and upset them each time they remember it.

It may churn around in the mind and manifest as ridiculous thoughts such as, 'look how he treated me. I'm far superior to him, I deserve more respect. I feel so humiliated,' and so on and so on in this fashion.

This is a true burden for us, a real weight to carry.

To live freely we have to leave the past to the past. We have to let go of the pain of insults and snide remarks, and be happy. After all, when we do remember these kinds of things it is ourselves who suffers again, not the other person. Perhaps they have completely forgotten the incident or were even not aware of it, but we carry the memory of the event with us like a lead weight. Let go!

We can also carry with us beautiful memories of a time gone by. A relationship, a first love, something wonderful. These actually are just the same. More burdens to carry.

When we remember too much from the past we use it to estimate and determine the future. When we spend our time making comparisons, we miss what is actually happening right now. We are always striving to create the perfect conditions for happiness.

We have to realise that whatever we carry becomes only a burden for ourselves.

In monastic communities there are many rules to govern behaviour, there have to be. So many people living together, each at their own level of spiritual progress. Some are more advanced than others and so need less rules to practice, whilst others need the guidance of the whole book!

In the Theravada tradition of Buddhism, where I spent some time as a monk, there are two hundred and twenty seven rules that monks must obey. This does not include some of the particular 'house rules' kept only by particular monasteries.

Monks have to lead a very disciplined life.

However, rules are valuable. They tell us how to behave in different circumstances when we don't know for ourselves. And this really is the point. When we don't know for ourselves, we need the guidance of a tried and tested external authority.

But here as always, we have to be careful. Many spiritual seekers outside the order of monks and nuns, become attached to rules and controlling systems without understanding them completely. When we are simply following instructions there can be the feeling of freedom because we are not making decisions for ourselves. Everything is taken care of for us. We don't have to make choices as to how to behave, we just follow the rules.

However, rules are not freedom. Rules are what we use in the path to freedom.

At one time there was a man who went to work in a factory, where his job was to sort potatoes. He was told to observe the potatoes as they came along a conveyor belt and to put the small ones in one sack, the medium-sized ones in another sack and the large ones in one in a third sack.

After two hours the man went to the office of the boss and said, "I quit!"

The boss was surprised and replied, "You quit? But the job is so easy!"

The man replied, "Yes the job is easy, but the decisions are killing me!"

Our own views and ideas of how things should be are simply more examples of the burdens that we carry with us. We bundle everything together, call it ourselves, and think that it is the truth. Then we try to persuade everyone else that only we have the right answers to life and that our way is the only way.

Once we can learn to see a view simply as a view, and an opinion simply as an opinion and not as ultimate truths, we will be able to pick them up when necessary, carry them for a while and use them if and when appropriate. Possibly even enjoy them and then lay them down again. Not spend our whole time looking for more things to carry.

We must know our own practice. This is the most important thing. Not to get caught up in rules and regulations or attachment to certain practices or meditation techniques. We have to know what is suitable to further our own spiritual advancement in this moment.

What works for someone else may not work for us, and so we must never compare what we are doing with another person.

When we listen with our heart, we will always know what is an appropriate action in any given circumstance. With this clear view we will respond with love and wisdom. From the perspective of worldly behaviour, our training is about learning to respond to the moment and let go of our habit of simply reacting.

The first monk in the story was a free man. He was free from the limiting idea that he was someone or something, and therefore had to behave in a particular way. His mind was not cluttered with views and opinions as to what right conduct was and so he was able to respond in the appropriate manner, and so help a fellow human being.

In life, there are many like a second monk, tied to rules and conditions, always doing what is expected and never really expressing themselves fully.

There are far fewer, like the first monk, completely free human beings.

Humility

'If we want to understand the real nature of existence
we have to go with humility to the truth
and listen to what it tells us.'

At one time there was a great Master living in Japan.
One day, the Governor of the city where the teacher lived, came to call. He presented his calling card to the attendant who took it straight to the Master. The Master read the card, it said 'Kitagaki, Governor of Kyoto'.
"I have no business with that fellow," said the Master, and handed the card back to his attendant.
The attendant in turn handed the card back to the Governor, with his apologies.
"Oh, that was my error," said the Governor, and with a pencil scratched out the words, 'Governor of Kyoto'.
The attendant took the now altered calling card back to the Master, and presented it to him.
This time the Master upon reading the card, smiled and said, "Oh, is that Kitagaki? Tell him to come in. I want to see that fellow."

In the world there are many different standards. Standards for the rich and standards for the poor. This is how it is. We find ourselves in a social situation, and then treat and get treated accordingly. In the West the standards are changing slowly, not all of us are still afraid of waiters and bank managers, but in the East things move more slowly.

In India is still very apparent. The social position, you are born into, you stay in. There may be many different social and cultural reasons for that, but the outcome is that you stay where you are and are expected to offer respect to those above you, whilst at the same time demanding respect from those below you. It is true that we all kick downward.

This is just a convention of course.
Actually, respect is something very special. It is not something that can be inherited as a birthright. In fact it is not something that can be related to social standing at all. Respect is a spiritual value, something given from one being to another, and established in an attitude of worthiness.
We offer our respect to those who are worthy, based not only in their understanding of the truth but also, and much more importantly, their demonstration of it. Understanding is never enough, it has to be lived. It has to be demonstrated.
So, in the world we have respect as social and spiritual conventions. However, if we examine those above and below us and then ourselves what do we find? What overwhelming truth do we experience?

We find that we are all exactly the same. From the lowest to the very highest in social circles. Convention apart we are all exactly the same.
We all suffer the problems and misfortunes of life. We all seek happiness, however we define that individually, and we all fear rejection and loneliness. From the moment we are born, we are subject to ageing, sickness and

eventually death. Not just some of us. Not only the poor and uneducated, but all of us. Each and every one.

And so when we come knocking on the door of truth, expecting to get past the Master, we had better be ready.

We have to leave all our baggage outside with our shoes, and enter with humility. This is the only way that we will get in. And who will meet us when we get our foot in the door of truth? Who will we find searching for the same things as we are?

We will find all our social superiors, inferiors and equals. But here we are all truly equal. Airs and graces will not help. Etiquette and social niceties have no value. Name dropping and social climbing, amount to nothing.

Here we are alone. In good company perhaps, but alone all the same.

The Masters demonstrate their compassion for the world by sharing their understanding. It would be easier sometimes for them to go and live quietly in a small cabin in the forest and far away from the many questions they have to face from the simply curious, but they stay within the public's reach and offer themselves. They demonstrate their compassion by staying in the world.

So when we approach a Master, we must be ready for a teaching, because this is all they can do. Share the truth with us.

When we are given a practice to help us enter through the door of truth, it is ourselves that has to do it. No matter what that practice is, whether it is formal meditation practice or simply a change in attitude towards our family, it is ourselves that has to do the work. This is something we can never delegate.

In meditation retreats, workshops and seminars, we are all in the same spiritual boat. We struggle and fight against some of the things that the mind presents, but this is exactly what the practice of spiritual development comes down to. The humble facing of ourselves alone, without outside help. Only we have the solution to our suffering and only we can do the work.

When you make your meditation practice, you really have to do it!

When you sit cross-legged on the floor with your eyes closed and your hands folded in your lap, you could be doing anything. You could be planning your next holiday or remembering the last one. You could be dreaming of winning the lottery this week, then you wouldn't have to do this. You would be rich and free from all the cares of life. You would be popular and socially in demand. Suddenly you would be free from the ravages of life, such as old age, sickness and death, and you would be able to be happy in a way never believed possible before. Your position in society would be elevated, and you would be respected by all. In fact, everything would be wonderful.

Nice try, but that's not how it works!

From Kings, Queens and governmental ministers down through the social ranks to the beggars and outcasts, the experience of life is the same for all of us, even if the quality of that experience is different.
We can say jokingly that the rich suffer in comfort, but actually, it is true.

We all suffer from the same manifestations of greed and aversions, wanting things to make us happy, and eradicating things we think are making us unhappy. This tendency sweeps over all beings, rich or not.

If we want to understand the real nature of existence we have to go with humility to the truth and listen to what it tells us. We have to leave our views, opinions and feelings of self-importance at the door. This is the baggage we cannot take with us.

The Master in the story knew exactly how to make a point. This is their role in life, to point! The Governor however was a good student. He was not confused by social convention. He knew where the truth was and how to approach it.

Super illusion
'Attachment is attachment,
and whatever we are attached to will hurt us'

At one time there was a famous Master, who had many disciples. This Master was also married and had a young family. One day, the youngest son of the Master died.
Soon after this tragic event, a disciple went to the home of the Master to receive a teaching. As he peered through the window he saw the Master sitting at the table crying at the loss of his young son. The disciple was shocked and angrily burst into the house where he confronted his teacher.
"What are you doing?" he yelled. "why are you crying, when you have told us so many times that everything is illusion?"
"Ah yes," replied the Master, "but this is super illusion."

This short story illustrates a beautiful Dhammic truth that confuses most spiritual seekers. Painful sensations are painful sensations, whether we have understanding or not. However, the subtle teaching is that we need to understand that the sensation is not the problem, only our attachment to it causes of suffering. Whatever has been conditioned by us in the past through our unenlightened behaviour, has to be experienced by us now in this moment or sometime in the future. Enlightened or not. It is inescapable. It is the law of Kamma and Vipaka[1], the law of cause and effect.

Our ignorance, manifesting as mental states and physical and verbal action based on greed, aversion and the general confusion as the to the reality of things, always comes back to haunt us. Even a practitioner so skilled that they no longer produce consequences for the future has to face the consequences of the past.

This is the spiritual secret.

This is where all our struggling and suffering really comes from. It is our thoughts, feelings and ideas from the past continually encroach upon our desire for happiness, right now. The more we suppress and try to force them away, the greater energy they develop to return.

This means that potentially painful feelings in the past, such as the attachment to one's own children will still be experienced as painful feelings now or in the future.

Attachment is attachment, and whatever we are attached to will hurt us.

It is only with the cultivation of wisdom that we can truly understand and accept this impersonal kammic cycle.

It is only with the cultivation of wisdom, that we will be able to recognise everything we experience as passing phenomenon.

Pleasant or unpleasant, happy or sad, difficult to endure or sheer delight.

Whatever arises passes away and is not what we really are.

---

[1] For further reading on Kamma and Vipaka, see: The Reality of Kamma in Daily Life, by Michael Kewley. Publshed by Pannadipa Books.

However our mind manifests in any moment, with wisdom we can be aware, but not trapped. We can enjoy the pleasant mental states, whilst having the ability to patiently endure the unpleasant ones.

Everything we experience has a cause, something empowered in the past, but if left to itself and not indulged or suppressed, it will pass by itself.

We don't have to push it away and we don't have to try to make it stay. With non-attached observation, acceptance and wisdom, we can truly know for ourselves where all our problems really begin and end. When we know this directly for ourselves we will allow the natural purification process of simply 'letting go' to begin.

When something painful arises in the mind, no matter what the cause, we can know it as painful. When something pleasant arises in the mind no matter what the cause, we can know it as pleasant. This is the simple truth that frees us from the bonds of pain and suffering.

The purpose of our spiritual life is the development of wisdom. Other than this our spiritual practice has no value. So learn to let go. Learn to be at peace with things as they are.

Learn to be in your life and be happy so you will share that happiness with all beings.

Simple daily meditation
'All our unhappiness and suffering comes from ourselves.'

At one time a student of a philosophical school of Buddhism went to study with a Dhamma Master. He stayed for many years and was a good student.
However, when he left, the Master warned him, "Studying the truth speculatively is a useful way of collecting teaching material, but remember that unless you meditate constantly, your light of truth may go out."

Although meditation is a word in common usage these days, it is still not something fully understood. There are many different types and styles of meditation, from simple relaxation exercises to the most profound practices of Insight Meditation (Vipassana), but whatever the style, they all require the same thing from you. Effort !
If you really want to change your life you yourself must make the effort, no-one can do it for you.

It is a fact that meditation established in the practices of awareness, love and acceptance, is the key to changing our life, because only through awareness and love can we transcend the stubborn illusion of 'self', and therefore the unhappiness that is part of this illusion. With awareness we are able to see and know the reality of this being that we call 'self' and with love and acceptance, we are able to be with this being without continually limiting it by applying conditions in every moment. The moment we apply conditions to ourselves we apply conditions to all beings.

Awareness then, is the tool we use in the direct and personal investigation of the cause of our unhappiness, often manifesting as stress, anger, fear, frustration and other unpleasant manifestations of mind. When we understand from our own direct experience, exactly where these things begin, we are in a position to finally do something about them, namely, let them go. Release ourselves from their grasp.

All our unhappiness and suffering comes from ourselves. It is always the reaction to a situation that causes our suffering, never the situation itself. The situation is just the situation. It is the reality of the moment. Our reaction or response to that reality will dictate our experience of peace or anxiety, happiness or unhappiness.

In other words:

The world we experience is the one that we create for ourselves,
moment after moment,
and this world is unique and personal to us.

No-one has the power to make you angry. Anger arises within us. No-one has the power to make you happy. Happiness arises within us. It is the same with all our mental states. With the cultivation of the practice of Loving Awareness we can begin to experience anger as something that is happening in the moment, but is not what we are. We can experience anger and not be angry. We can experience fear, and not be afraid. We can experience depression and not be depressed.

Loving Awareness is the path we each have to walk. To see the mind and not be afraid. To know the mind and not to judge ourselves for its content. To let go of our continual, habitual and limiting identification with this mind as being who, and what we are.

The mind is not what we are, it is only that which we become.
When we stop 'becoming' these endless and ever changing mental states we will be free, and our lives will express that freedom. A life where we no longer feel ourselves to be the victim, but rather the master.
A life of love, joy and peace. A life that is a blessing to ourselves and all the beings, human and other that we share the world with.

Simple Awareness Meditation[2]

Sit comfortably in a chair and let the eyes close naturally. Awareness is a condition of the mind, not of physical posture, so it is not necessary to sit 'Buddha' style on the floor, unless you are able to do so comfortably. Keep the back straight , and without tension. Let your hands rest in your lap and place your feet flat on the floor. Do not allow the head to fall forward, but maintain an elegant posture. Imagine someone will take your photograph whilst you are meditating, so maintain the best and most beautiful posture you can.

---

2   For complete instructions into Vipassana and Loving Kindness Meditation see: Vipassana – the way to an awakened life. by Michael Kewley. Published by Pannadipa Books.

Without trying to control the breathing in any way, take your awareness to the breath as you experience it in the nostrils. Don't follow it down into the chest or abdomen, and don't try to visualise it leaving the body but keep your attention firmly fixed at the nose.

Relax, but stay alert. In time you will begin to feel the subtle sensation of breath as it enters and leaves the nostrils. Stay with this. When thoughts arise simply notice them. Don't follow them, push them away or change them, just be patient and gentle and return the attention to the breath. The same applies any emotion or sensation you may experience in the body. Notice, accept without judgement and return to the breath.

If you must move during the meditation (to scratch an itch for example) use that whole movement as a part of the meditation, not something outside to distract you. It may seem contrary, but everything is here to help us. Keeping your eyes closed, put your attention in the hand and move slowly to scratch the itch. Feel the weight of the hand, notice any sensations, notice whatever can be noticed. Scratch the itch with awareness, return the hand slowly to your lap and the attention to the breath. In this way everything becomes the meditation, and eventually we take this attitude into our daily life.

Decide in advance how long you will meditate for and be determined to adhere to this time. However, fifteen or twenty minutes is enough in daily life and when the time is finished leave the meditation slowly and mindfully, not trying to hold on to a peaceful state of mind, but just being aware, and ready for the next moment of your life.

The best way to end the meditation sitting is by incorporating the beautiful the practice known as Metta

Bhavana or Loving Kindness. As with all styles of meditation, there are many variations of this practice but the essential quality is to open the heart and radiate love, compassion and acceptance to all beings.

Repeat mentally, emphasising the beautiful power of these words, three or four times;

> May I accept other beings exactly as they are in this moment.
> May I accept this moment exactly as it is.
> May I accept myself exactly as I am in this moment.

This simple yet powerful practice allows all our judgements of ourselves and others to fall away, so that we can be at peace with everyone and everything, even if we don't like them or approve of what they do.

To practice in this way each day will bring good results. A way of living and being in the world that is established in balance and wisdom, and the natural ability to accept and then respond to life as it unfolds moment after moment. True power and true strength is always through awareness and love. Without with awareness and love, we are simply the victim to life.

But remember, consistency is everything. The more we practice the more we receive the results of that practice.

> May all beings be happy

Acknowledgements

No book ever writes itself, and although the idea always seems simple, the actual work of sharing ones thoughts in a coherent way demands the help of others.

In this respect I feel blessed to have been aided by the people listed below, for their help, support and expertise.

Sandra and Bill Burtonwood, who through their kindness and generosity, made available the very first edition.

Isabelle Kewley, my wife, supporter and friend, who typeset the words and made them into the book you are holding.

To all my students and disciples for their encouragement to continually make the Pure Dhamma available so that all beings may benefit.

To these people and others I have not mentioned, I am as always, extremely grateful.

May they all be well and happy

Higher Than Happiness

About the author

Michael Kewley is the former Buddhist monk Paññadipa, who is now an internationally acclaimed Master of Dhamma, presenting courses and meditation retreats throughout the world. For many years he was the guiding teacher at the International Meditation Centre, Budh Gaya, India and is the founder of the Pure Dhamma tradition of spiritual awakening and the Being Awake meditation group network.

A disciple of the late Sayadaw Rewata Dhamma, he teaches solely on the instruction of his own Master; to share the Dhamma, in the spirit of the Buddha, so that all beings might benefit. On 26th May 2002, during a special ceremony at the Dhamma Talaka Temple in England, he was awarded the title of Dhammachariya.

A full biography of Michael Kewley, including videos and Dhamma talk extracts, can be found at:

www.puredhamma.org

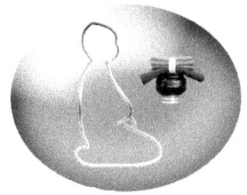

Also by Michael Kewley

Published by Pannadipa Books

    Vipassana: the way to an awakened life
    Not This
    Life Changing Magic
    Walking the Path
    The Other Shore
    The reality of Kamma
    Life is not personal
    Buttons in the Dana box
    The Dhammapada

German translation:

    Mehr als nur glücklich sein
    Vipassana: Der Weg in ein erwachtes Leben
    Nimm das Leben nicht persönlich
    Knöpfe in der Dana Box

www.ingramcontent.com/pod-product-compliance
Ingram Content Group UK Ltd.
Pitfield, Milton Keynes, MK11 3LW, UK
UKHW021257180426
11947UKWH00015B/892